The Causes of the Civil War

Dale Anderson

WORLD ALMANAC® LIBRARY

Please visit our web site at: www.worldalmanaclibrary.com
For a free color catalog describing World Almanac® Library's
list of high-quality books and multimedia programs,
call 1-800-848-2928 (USA) or 1-800-387-3178 (Canada).
World Almanac® Library's fax: (414) 332-3567.

Library of Congress Cataloging-in-Publication Data

Anderson, Dale, 1953-
    The causes of the Civil War / by Dale Anderson.
        p. cm. — (World Almanac Library of the Civil War)
    Includes bibliographical references and index.
    ISBN 0-8368-5581-7 (lib. bdg.)
    ISBN 0-8368-5590-6 (softcover)
    1. United States—History—Civil War, 1861-1865—Causes—
Juvenile literature. 2. Slavery—Southern States—History—Juvenile
literature. 3. United States—Politics and government—1849-1861—
Juvenile literature. [1. United States—History—Civil War, 1861-1865—
Causes. 2. Slavery—History. 3. United States—Politics and govern-
ment—1849-1861.] I. Title. II. Series.
E459.A55   2004
973.7'11—dc22   2003062487

First published in 2004 by
World Almanac® Library
330 West Olive Street, Suite 100
Milwaukee, WI 53212 USA

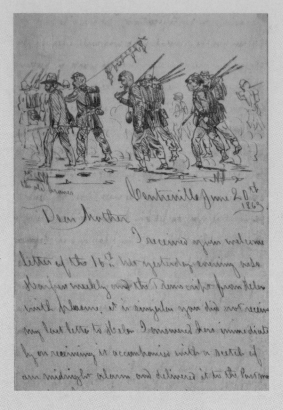

Produced by Discovery Books
Project editor: Geoff Barker
Editor: Geoff Barker
Designer and page production: Laurie Shock, Shock Design, Inc.
Photo researcher: Rachel Tisdale
Consultant: Andrew Frank, Assistant Professor of History, Florida
        Atlantic University
Maps: Stefan Chabluk
World Almanac® editorial direction: Mark Sachner
World Almanac® art direction: Tammy Gruenewald

Photo credits: American Pictures: cover, pp. 9, 10, 14, 15 (left), 18, 22,
23, 24, 25 29, 35, 38, 42; Library of Congress: title page, pp. 2, 27;
Bettmann/Corbis: pp. 5, 11, 13, 19, 20, 21, 28, 41; The Granger
Collection, New York: p. 6; Corbis: pp. 15 (right), 33, 36, 37, 40; Peter
Newark's Peter Newark's Military Pictures: p. 30; Medford Historical
Society Collection/Corbis: p. 43.

Printed in the United States of America

1 2 3 4 5 6 7 8 9 08 07 06 05 04

**Cover: When it was time for slaves to pick cotton, even
women and children were sent to the fields to work.**

*"To my mother, who got me
Bruce Catton; my brother,
who shared my passion for the
Civil War; and my wife and
sons, who cheerfully put up
with several field trips and
countless anecdotes."*

— DALE ANDERSON

Contents

CHAPTER ONE

A Divided Country

*"The . . . destiny of the
American field is to subdue the continent—
to rush over this vast field to the Pacific Ocean— . . .
to set the principle of self-government at work— . . . to
establish a new order in human affairs— . . . to teach old
nations a new civilization—to confirm the destiny of the human
race—to carry the career of mankind to its culminating
point— . . . to perfect science—to emblazon history with the
conquest of peace—to shed a new and resplendent glory
upon mankind. . . . Divine task! Immortal mission!*

William Gilpin, report to Congress (1846)

Looking Back: The United States in 1850

At the beginning of 1850, the United States was an energetic, growing nation. It had recently expanded greatly, adding to its territory all of present-day Texas, California, Utah, Nevada, Oregon, Washington, and Idaho and most of Arizona, New Mexico, and Colorado. And these new lands paid off quick dividends when gold was discovered in California in 1848.

The population was growing, too. From 1840 to 1850, the number of U.S. citizens jumped from 17.1 million to 23.2 million. Contributing to this growth was a stream of immigrants that poured into the country. More than 1.7 million people came to the United States between 1841 and 1850.

They came because the U.S. economy was booming. Farmers were harvesting more and more food. In 1850, they produced 592 million bushels of corn and 100 million bushels of wheat. Nearly 2.5 million bales of U.S. cotton kept the textile machines humming both in New England and abroad in Great

Spurred by the spread of the railroad, Chicago, Illinois, was a growing city in the 1850s.

Britain. U.S. merchant ships plied the seas. Railroads were spreading, making it faster to move goods and people across the expanding country.

With all this success and promise, Americans in 1850 had much to be optimistic about. Many spoke of the country's **manifest destiny**—the belief that the United States would expand across the continent to the Pacific Ocean. William Gilpin reflected this belief in his 1846 report to Congress about western lands. In a land bustling with activity, people looked with hope to a bright future.

A Deeply Divided Country

But the United States was also a deeply divided nation—in some ways, less a single country than a gathering of sections. Those sections differed in many ways. The North and the South clashed over several issues. One of the key issues they struggled over was what shape the new lands in the west of the country would take. In those differences— and in the mistrust and anger that had built up over several decades— lay the very roots of the Civil War.

These mills in Lowell, Massachusetts, were the major center of the U.S. textile industry.

The North

The section of the country called the **North** included the states from Maine south to Pennsylvania, west along the Ohio River to Iowa, and north to the Canadian border. This region was the country's industrial powerhouse. Workers in Massachusetts made textiles and shoes. Connecticut turned out clocks as well as firearms. Western Pennsylvania produced iron. Northern factories attracted growing numbers of workers to cities. In fact, twelve of the country's twenty largest cities were in the North, with New York City topping the list with nearly 700,000 people.

Northern businesses, competing with those in Europe, wanted the government to pass **tariffs**. Tariffs, or duties, are amounts added to the cost of goods imported from other countries. Foreign tariffs made U.S. products seem cheaper and as a result more desirable.

Northern business owners also liked projects that improved transportation. They wanted the government to build roads and canals, and they invested in railroads and ships. These improvements made it cheaper to get their goods to market.

Of course, not all Northerners were factory owners—or even factory workers. Most Northerners farmed. Many had small holdings and grew only enough food for their families. In parts of Pennsylvania and the **Old Northwest**, though, farmers took advantage of rich soil and long growing

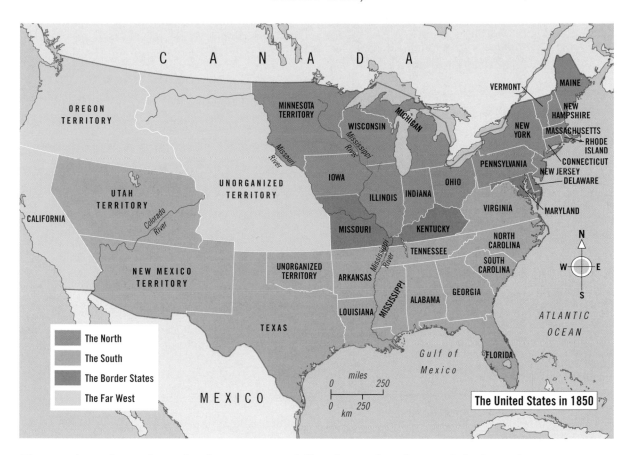

The number of people in the four sections differed greatly. The North had nearly 60 percent of the nation's people. The South had just over a third, but a large number of them were enslaved African Americans. The Border States had only 6 percent of the people; nearly one in six of them were slaves. The Far West had less than 1 percent of the country's people.

seasons to produce extra food, which they shipped east or south.

The people of the North were mostly descended from **immigrants** from the British Isles. The great majority were Protestants, but the 1840s and 1850s saw a surge in immigration of Irish Catholics. They tended to settle in cities, especially in New Jersey, New York, and the New England states. Some Scandinavians and many Germans also immigrated to the North

in these years. Germans generally lived in the areas around Cincinnati, Milwaukee, and St. Louis. Most Scandinavians settled on farms in the western part of the old Northwest.

Many of the people who lived along the Ohio River had moved there from the South. They also relied on the Ohio and Mississippi rivers to get their crops to market. As a result, they had some economic and personal ties to the South.

LIFE IN THE 1850s

Americans lived very differently in the 1850s than they do today. There were no cars; people got around by animal power, by boat or train, or on foot. There was no electricity. They heated themselves with fires, and if they got too hot, they opened the windows. Most people earned their living by physical labor of some kind. Most people farmed, spending large parts of the year plowing, sowing seed, weeding, and harvesting. Women worked hard washing clothes by hand and making things like soap and candles that the family needed but could not be bought.

The great majority of people lived in rural areas, not cities. In the North, nearly three-quarters of all people lived in rural areas. In the South, nine in ten people lived outside cities. Most cities were quite small. While New York had nearly 700,000 people, only five others topped 100,000. Only one of these cities, the busy port of New Orleans, was in the South.

The South

The **South** included the states from Virginia west to Arkansas and south to the Gulf of Mexico. These states had slavery, which the Northern states had made illegal by 1850. Differences over slavery became a major cause of the Civil War.

In 1850, nearly 9.5 million people lived in the South. Of that number, nearly 3 million were enslaved African Americans. These slaves were a major source of labor in the South. The South, with few factories, based its economy on agriculture. While some farmers simply grew food for their families, large landowners used slave labor to grow **cash crops** on large **plantations** for export.

Not all Southern whites owned slaves. Many farmers were too poor to invest in slaves or had land that was not suited to cash crops. Some owned just a few slaves. Only a small number of Southern whites owned large numbers of slaves.

This small number of plantation owners, though, dominated Southern society and politics. They were the South's social elite—more educated, wealthier, and more powerful than the ordinary farmer. They typically ran the state governments—and were an important political force in Washington, D.C., as well.

They used that power to push for policies that helped them. With little industry in the region, Southerners had to buy manufactured goods made elsewhere, often from abroad. As a result, they did not want tariffs imposed on imported manufactured goods—the

When it was time for slaves to pick cotton, even women and children were sent to the fields to work.

duties that benefited the North hurt them. So they opposed tariffs. They also had less interest in internal improvements like railroads. High on their political agenda, though, was the protection of slavery, which Southerners called their "peculiar institution."

The Border States

Between the North and South were the **Border States**—Delaware, Maryland, Kentucky, and Missouri. They had characteristics of both sections. There was industry, as in the North. But these states also had slavery, linking them to the South.

The Far West

The **Far West** was sparsely settled. California, with nearly 93,000 people, had more than half of the region's population, many of whom had just reached the state following the gold rush of 1848. Present-day New Mexico and Arizona—and to some extent California—had large Spanish-speaking populations. Most of the West, though, was still home to Native Americans.

CHAPTER TWO

The "Peculiar Institution"

~

Enslaved African Americans were offered for sale at slave auctions. There was no guarantee that the same person would purchase both husband and wife. The Southerners called slavery their "peculiar institution."

Ending Slavery in the North

When the United States was founded, slavery existed in the Northern states as well as in the Southern ones. It was never such an important economic or social institution in the North, however. By 1850, it had been banned from New England to Pennsylvania, including in New York and New Jersey.

Slavery did not exist in the Old Northwest. When this area was organized as a territory in the 1780s, Congress banned slavery from it. Though some Southerners moved to the region, they were typically poorer, non-slaveholding farmers, not the wealthy people who owned slaves.

Slavery and Cotton

Slavery, known as their "peculiar institution," flourished in the South. Slaves were used to grow cotton, tobacco, rice, and indigo.

In the early 1800s, slavery spread rapidly. The growing British textile industry needed cotton. The South had the right soil and climate to grow it. But the South produced little cotton because it took so long for people to separate the seeds from the fiber. In the 1790s, New Englander Eli Whitney invented a machine—the cotton gin—to do this work. Suddenly, a slave could clean fifty pounds of cotton a day instead of only one pound by hand.

FREE BLACKS IN THE NORTH

By the 1850s, African Americans were free in the North, but there were few of them. Of the North's 13.3 million people, fewer than 200,000—merely 1.5 percent—were black.

Although Northern blacks were free, they did not have equality. Blacks suffered from discrimination and prejudice. They found it difficult to find the jobs they wanted or to get an education. They also did not enjoy the full rights of American citizens. Whites' feelings against blacks sometimes erupted in violent riots that left blacks' homes burned.

Workers feed cotton into a cotton gin, which separates the seeds from the fiber.

WALKER'S APPEAL

As cotton growing spread, slavery became more deeply entrenched in the South. At the same time, criticism of slavery grew. A powerful critique of slavery was written in 1829 by David Walker, a free black who had left North Carolina for Boston.

Walker's Appeal to the Colored Citizens of the World blasted slavery as a moral outrage. He urged whites to free slaves—and warned that they must fear for their lives if they did not. He implored slaves across the South to revolt. He scoffed at the idea that, once freed, African Americans should be sent back to colonies in Africa. "America," he told whites, "is as much our country, as it is yours." To make sure his message got through, Walker recruited sailors to bring copies of his book to southern ports, hoping that they would circulate among slaves.

"King Cotton"

Southern farmers began to grow more and more cotton. With their profits, they bought more land—and more slaves—so they could grow even more. Cotton growing spread into new areas, including Alabama, Mississippi, Arkansas, and Texas. Production mushroomed from 100,000 bales in 1801 to 2.4 million bales in 1849. Planters believed that cotton would drive the world's new industrial economy, and they began calling their crop "King Cotton."

The Lives of African Americans

Of course, the planters' success was made possible by forcing slaves to do the tiring, grueling work. Some slaves worked in the master's house. Some learned skills like blacksmithing. Most, though, were field hands, working from sunup until sundown. They hoed the land and planted the seeds. They tended the crops and pulled weeds. Come harvest time, they did the back-breaking work of picking the cotton. They did this work under the watchful eye of the owner or an overseer. Those who were not working hard enough could be whipped or punished in other ways.

Slaveholders controlled slaves' lives. They decided where the slaves lived, what they ate, and what clothes they wore. They could separate husbands from wives and parents from children simply by sending one member of a family to another plantation—or by selling him or her to someone in a distant state.

Resistance, Rebellion, and Flight

Slaves suffered from the lack of freedom, the pressure of forced labor, the breakup of families, and many other cruelties. But African Americans did not simply accept this fate. They found ways to resist. They worked slowly or **sabotaged** equipment. Some tried to fight their way to freedom. But rebels were killed—often in public—to warn other slaves not to try the same thing.

Many slaves ran away, using a secret network called the "Underground Railroad." Free blacks and some whites helped them reach freedom in the North and Canada. Harriet Tubman—herself an escaped slave—freed as many as 300 slaves in this way.

Harriet Tubman (far left, holding a pan) posed with a group of African Americans she helped rescue from slavery.

Abolitionists

From the 1830s through the 1850s, **abolitionists** campaigned to outlaw slavery. Speakers like Wendell Phillips and Theodore Parker lectured crowds on slavery's evils. William Lloyd Garrison denounced slavery in his newspaper *The Liberator*. Many of these antislavery crusaders were women, like the sisters Angelina and Sarah Grimké. Many, too, were African Americans. The escaped slave Frederick Douglass was renowned for his powerful speaking style and eloquence.

The South Responds

Abolitionists' verbal attacks angered Southerners. They said that abolishing slavery would deprive them of their property. Southern writers argued that African Americans were happy as slaves. They contrasted the care that slaves received to the harsh treatment of "wage slaves" working in Northern factories. Southerners also attacked the abolitionists. Some states offered rewards for their arrest. Crowds sometimes seized abolitionist books and newspapers. Postmasters in the South removed such writings from the mail.

In the first issue of *The Liberator* in January 1831, William Lloyd Garrison announced that he would push for immediate freedom for all slaves and concluded, "I will be heard." This front page is from an edition nearly thirty years later.

Some illustrations made slavery look almost pleasant, ignoring the harsh realities.

"Free laborers have less liberty than slaves, are worse paid and provided for, and have no valuable rights. Slaves . . . are secure in the enjoyment of all their rights, which provide for their physical comfort at all times and under all circumstances. The free laborer must be employed or starved, yet no one is obliged to employ him."

Virginian George Fitzhugh,
Cannibals All! (1857)

FREDERICK DOUGLASS

Born on a plantation in Maryland, Frederick Douglass was separated from his mother while young. As a youth, he taught himself to read and write. In his twenties, he escaped, settled in Massachusetts, and married. In his thirties, he joined the abolitionist movement.

Douglass became a leading spokesman for African Americans. His **autobiography**, published in 1845, revealed the story of his escape. This put Douglass in danger of being captured and returned to slavery. He fled to Europe, where he stayed for two years speaking out against slavery. In that time, he earned enough to buy his freedom. He returned to the United States and started an antislavery newspaper, The North Star.

After the Civil War began, he pushed President Abraham Lincoln to free the slaves. He continued to work in reform movements until his death in 1889.

CHAPTER THREE

Slavery in the Territories

Balancing Free and Slave States

In the 1800s, slavery became a political issue between North and South. The key issue was representation in the Senate. For many years, free states and slave states had an equal number of senators. This balance meant that Congress could not pass laws either harming slavery or promoting it.

In 1803, buying the Louisiana Territory from France added many lands west of the Mississippi River. The 1848 peace ending the Mexican War added still more western lands. At first, these areas were territories, but eventually

When passed in 1820, the Missouri Compromise seemed to settle the issue of the spread of slavery by banning it in territories north of Missouri's southern border.

they would become states. The question was, would they be free states or slave states?

The Missouri Compromise

The question first arose in 1819, when Missouri applied for statehood. Its constitution allowed slavery, which would upset the balance then in the Senate. Congress held up granting statehood for more than a year until a compromise could be found.

Henry Clay, Speaker of the House, fashioned a deal. In this agreement, both Missouri and Maine were admitted as new states. Because one was a slave state and the other was a free state, the balance in the Senate was maintained.

Another part of the compromise bill banned slavery in the future from any territory north of the southern boundary of Missouri. This "Missouri Compromise line," or 36°30' line, would play an important role in the debate over slavery in the territories in future years.

Growing Southern Anger

The Missouri Compromise of 1820 settled the issue of slavery in the territories for thirty years. But disagreements still flared between North and South. One flashpoint arose in 1828, when Congress passed high tariffs despite Southern objections.

The legislature of South Carolina was outraged by the tariff. It passed a law declaring the tariff "null and void" in the state. The legislature vowed to **secede** if the federal government tried to collect the tariffs in its harbors. It was a direct challenge to the authority of the federal government.

The threat of military action to enforce the law and a new compromise that Clay fashioned settled this "Nullification Crisis." But the threat of secession remained. Southerners threatened to leave the Union several times over the following years. Some abolitionists said the North should secede to remove the moral stain of slavery.

The Wilmot Proviso

The issue of slavery in the territories reappeared in the 1840s. U.S. victories in Mexican War battles made it increasingly likely that the United States would win new lands from Mexico. David Wilmot, a congressman from Pennsylvania, introduced an amendment to a bill that would ban slavery from any of these new lands. Though the Senate blocked Wilmot's amendment, strong Northern support for his move signaled that difficult times lay ahead.

The Compromise of 1850

In 1850, California applied for statehood as a free state. There was no

In January 1850, Henry Clay presented his plan for the Compromise of 1850 to the Senate. Listening are South Carolina's John Calhoun (standing second from right) and Daniel Webster (seated on the left of picture, with his head resting in his left hand).

ready solution like that used in 1820— this time, there were no territories with slavery that were also prepared for statehood.

Eventually Congress settled on a new compromise. In it, California was admitted as a free state. At the same time, the newly acquired areas of Arizona, New Mexico, and Utah were organized into territories that could contain slavery if the majority of the people in each area wanted it. The principle was called "popular sovereignty"—the people, who are the ultimate power in a democracy, would settle the issue of slavery in a given area.

John C. Calhoun of South Carolina spoke bitterly against the deal, which he said did not protect the South. Daniel Webster of Massachusetts backed it, saying "I speak today for the preservation of the Union." Congress passed the compromise agreement.

This agreement broke the Missouri Compromise. Utah, north of the Missouri Compromise line, could now have slavery. The people of Arizona and New Mexico, south of the line, could now reject it. The chief effect of the agreement, though, was to sow mistrust between North and South.

HENRY CLAY

Born in Virginia in 1777, Henry Clay moved to Kentucky at age 21 to practice law. Soon after, he entered politics. He served at various times as a representative, a senator, Speaker of the House, and secretary of state. However, he never achieved his dream of becoming president. Nevertheless, he was one of the most powerful political leaders of the period between 1800 and 1850. His strong speeches against Great Britain helped propel the United States into the War of 1812. His "American Plan" of building canals, supporting a national bank, and creating tariffs to promote U.S. industry became the central program of the Whig party. The Whigs were one of the two main political parties in the United States from the mid-1830s to the mid-1850s.

Clay gained the title "the Great Compromiser" for his role in fashioning the two major pieces of legislation that calmed, for a short time at least, tensions between the North and South. Those were the Missouri Compromise of 1820 and the Compromise of 1850. In both actions, his guiding principle was to preserve the Union. He died just two years after the 1850 compromise, spared the pain that the Civil War would doubtless have caused him.

CHAPTER FOUR

The Bloodshed Begins

The Fugitive Slave Act

A key part of the Compromise of 1850 was a tough new law making it easier for slaveholders to capture fugitive, or escaped, slaves. It also made it a crime to block the return of runaways. In fact, the law compelled law enforcement officers in the North to help return them—something they had often resisted doing. "Slave catchers" quickly went North and in little over a year seized nearly one hundred African Americans. A few were later released, but most were taken south as fugitives.

These seizures outraged many Northerners. In some cases, crowds led by abolitionists prevented slave catchers from doing their work. Southerners protested bitterly. Meanwhile, several thousand blacks fled the North for Canada.

Uncle Tom's Cabin

Among the angry Northerners was Harriet Beecher Stowe. Daughter of one minister and wife of another, she felt that slavery and the return of fugitive slaves violated Christian morality. She wrote a groundbreaking novel to expose the outrages of slavery. Stowe said that she wanted to make "this whole nation feel what an accursed thing slavery is." Published in 1852, *Uncle Tom's Cabin* sold more than 300,000 copies in the first year alone.

A bookseller announces the sale of several editions of Stowe's controversial and high-selling novel.

Stowe's book was not an anti-Southern attack. Some Southern characters are sympathetic, and the vicious overseer who abuses slaves comes from New England. But Stowe's vivid scenes highlighted the cruel inhumanity of slavery. The central character, the slave Uncle Tom, is presented as a Christian martyr.

The Sectional Divide

Stowe's book fueled passions. Southern audiences blasted it as a slander. A New Orleans newspaper declared, "There never before was anything so detestable or so monstrous among women" as Stowe. Some suggested banning the book in the South. Yet the copies that reached the region sold quickly. Abolitionists hailed the book as a triumph. Northern audiences were upset by the glimpse into the horrors of slavery.

In 1854, slave catchers moved into Boston to seize another fugitive. When abolitionists resisted, the federal government had to call in troops to enforce the law. Soon after, Massachusetts and several other Northern states passed "personal liberty laws." These laws essentially nullified the Fugitive Slave Act within certain state boundaries. Southerners protested once again, but the new state laws stuck.

HARRIET BEECHER STOWE

Born in New England, Harriet Beecher received a solid education. In her early twenties, she moved with her family to Cincinnati, Ohio, where she married and had several children. She also wrote occasional short stories. In the nearby state of Kentucky, she saw slavery firsthand and was appalled. She wrote Uncle Tom's Cabin *at her sister's suggestion. "I will if I live," Stowe promised.*

Stowe wrote another antislavery novel in the 1850s and many other books during the rest of her life. When Abraham Lincoln met her in 1862, he remarked, "So this is the little woman who wrote the book that made this great war."

The Kansas-Nebraska Act

In the midst of the turmoil over the Fugitive Slave Act, the issue of slavery in the territories reappeared. In 1853, Stephen A. Douglas of Illinois wrote a bill to organize Kansas and Nebraska as territories. To win Southern support, Douglas had to agree to open these territories to slavery. He included language that repealed the Missouri Compromise. After bitter debate, the bill was passed in 1854. But trouble followed.

"Bleeding Kansas"

First came the outbreak of violence in Kansas. The new bill used the "popular sovereignty" idea, allowing the people of the territories to decide whether to have slavery or not. The result was disastrous. Both proslavery and antislavery forces sent settlers into Kansas. The two sides quickly began to fight.

The violence worsened in May 1856. First proslavery forces looted and pillaged Lawrence, a town of antislav-

A group of antislavery Kansans stands by their cannon near the town of Lawrence in 1856.

ery settlers. Then a small force led by abolitionist John Brown seized five proslavery settlers and executed them. This event came to be called the Pottawatomie Massacre, after the creek where the killings took place. Southerners protested once again.

The army eventually restored order in Kansas, but about 200 people had died in "Bleeding Kansas."

The Rise of the Republican Party

Another result of the Kansas-Nebraska Act was to destroy the two-party system that had existed for several decades. For years, Whigs and Democrats had struggled for control of the Congress and the presidency. Both parties had enjoyed support in both the North and the South. The Kansas-Nebraska Act left both badly damaged.

The Democrats were deeply split. Northern Democrats grew frustrated at the hard-line proslavery position of the Southern Democrats. Some left the party, although the majority hung on. Southern Democrats, meanwhile, no longer trusted Democrats from the North.

The Whig party simply collapsed. Southern Whigs—increasingly focused on defending slavery— left the party, many joining the Democratic party. Northern Whigs left, too. Many of them helped form

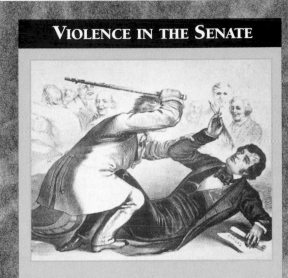

VIOLENCE IN THE SENATE

As Kansas decided whether or not to have slavery, and the two sides started to fight, Charles Sumner of Massachusetts gave a speech in the Senate blaming Southerners for "the crime against Kansas." Two days later, South Carolina Congressman Preston Brooks approached Sumner at his Senate desk. Brooks was offended by Sumner's harsh criticism of a South Carolina senator who was his relative. Brooks hit Sumner repeatedly on the head with his gold-tipped cane. It was now the Northerners' turn to take offense.

the new Republican party. The Republicans backed many of the causes that had been popular with the Whigs, but they also took a strong antislavery stand that made them unpopular in the South.

The Election of 1856

The new party first appeared on the national scene in the election of 1856. The Democrats united—one last time—behind James Buchanan of Pennsylvania. The Republicans offered up John C. Frémont, a well-known explorer and a dashing figure.

Frémont polled nearly 1.4 million votes and 114 electoral votes. Though he received fewer votes than Buchanan, the Republicans still made a strong showing for a first election. But Frémont won only states in the North. The Republican party was clearly a **sectional** party. Buchanan added a few key northern states to a solid South and became president.

Dred Scott was actually freed by his owner a few months after the Supreme Court ruled against him.

The Dred Scott Decision

Buchanan had barely taken office when another crisis arose. Two African-American slaves—Dred Scott and his wife Harriet—sued for their freedom. They argued that since they had been taken north of the Missouri Compromise line—to free soil—they should be free. In 1857 the Supreme Court, dominated by Southerners, ruled against them. The Court went further, saying that Congress had acted unconstitutionally when it banned slavery from any territories. Slaves were property, the Court said, and Congress did not have the right to take people's property.

The decision dismayed many Northerners. Some feared that the logical conclusion was that no state could ban slavery.

"On the subject of slavery, the North and South . . . are not only two Peoples, but they are rival, hostile Peoples."

Charleston Mercury (1858)

Thomas Hovenden's painting *Last Moments of John Brown* shows the abolitionist on his way to be hanged.

John Brown Strikes

Two years later, violence erupted again. Abolitionist John Brown and some associates seized an **arsenal** in Harper's Ferry, Virginia. They hoped to provoke a slave revolt, but none developed. Buchanan sent army troops, who captured Brown and the others. Brown was quickly tried for breaking Virginia law. Found guilty of treason, he was hanged. In his last speech at the trial, Brown declared himself willing to "forfeit my life for the furtherance of the ends of justice."

Abolitionists viewed him as a hero. To Southerners, he was a villain. The fact that Northerners glorified him helped to convince many Southerners that they were no longer welcome in the Union. As one Richmond newspaper wrote, "Thousands of men . . . who, a month ago, scoffed at the idea of a dissolution of the Union . . . now hold the opinion that its days are numbered."

In this climate of growing anger and frustration, a new presidential election loomed. The election of 1860 would be a fateful one.

CHAPTER FIVE

The Election of 1860

*"When this Government
was first established, it was the policy of its
founders to prohibit the spread of slavery into the new
Territories of the United States. . . . But [Senator] Douglas and his
friends have broken up that policy, and placed [slavery] upon a new
basis by which it is to become national and perpetual. All I have asked . . .
is that it should be placed back again upon the basis that the fathers of
our Government originally placed it upon. I have no doubt that it
would become extinct . . . if we but . . . [restrict]
it from the new Territories."*

Abraham Lincoln, speech in Jonesboro, Illinois (September 1858)

The Emergence of Lincoln

One of the candidates in the 1860 presidential election was Illinois lawyer Abraham Lincoln. At this time, Lincoln had an unremarkable political career. He had served four terms in the Illinois legislature and one in the U.S. House of Representatives. Then he lost a bid for the Senate in 1858.

But that losing campaign had thrust him into the national limelight. Lincoln had run that year against Stephen A. Douglas. Since Douglas was likely to be the Democrats' presidential nominee in 1860, many eyes watched his Senate campaign. Republican Lincoln benefited from the attention, winning a reputation as firmly opposed to the spread of slavery but moderate enough to allow it to continue in the South. He was known as a self-made man who had risen from humble origins, and he was seen as honest.

Two years later, the Republicans were looking for their own presidential candidate. Several party leaders hoped to win the nomination, but each had problems that made him unlikely to win election in November. Lincoln had none of those problems. He also profited from having shrewd campaign managers and a crowd of thousands of supporters at the party convention held in his home state of Illinois. In May 1860, the Republicans picked him as their nominee.

THE LINCOLN-DOUGLAS DEBATES

Lincoln gained fame in 1858 from the series of debates he held with Douglas. The two candidates appeared together in several towns in Illinois, where they detailed their views on the day's issues— principally on the question of slavery in the territories. In one debate, Lincoln cornered Douglas into saying that the people of a territory could exclude slavery simply by failing to pass laws that would enforce it. That statement—called the Freeport Doctrine—cost Douglas vital Southern support in the 1860 election.

STEPHEN A. DOUGLAS

Born in Vermont in 1813, Stephen A. Douglas became a lawyer and moved to Illinois in his twenties. In just a few years, he was named to the Illinois Supreme Court, a remarkable achievement for someone so young.

Douglas became a leader in the state Democratic party and by 1848 was serving in the U.S. Senate. There he skillfully helped win passage of the Compromise of 1850. But he was unable to steer a moderate course through the rising sectional passions of the 1850s.

After losing the 1860 election, Douglas watched sadly as the nation split as well. He backed Lincoln's efforts to restore the Union, but died in 1861.

A Party Fractures

While the Republican convention proceeded smoothly, the Democrats had serious trouble. They met in Charleston, South Carolina, in late April. Southern delegates insisted that the party support slavery in the territories. Northern Democrats, who outnumbered them, voted the idea down. Several Southerners left the convention, and the remainder refused to support Douglas as the nominee. When the convention failed to name a candidate after 57 ballots, it decided to adjourn and meet six weeks later in Baltimore, Maryland.

At the Baltimore convention, Douglas won his nomination, but the party split into two sectional branches. Large numbers of Southerners walked out. They met separately and nominated John C. Breckinridge of Kentucky.

Four-Way Race

There was one more candidate in 1860. A small group of conservative former Whigs from both North and South formed a new party, the Constitutional Union party. They nominated John Bell, a Tennessee slaveholder who had not pushed for the spread of slavery in the territories. The party claimed to "recognize no political principle other than the Constitution . . . the Union . . . and the Enforcement of the Laws." Although the party had

During the 1860 campaign, Republicans formed "Wide-Awake clubs." Uniformed members marched in parades like this one in New York City to promote Lincoln's candidacy.

The Election of 1860

CANDIDATE	PARTY	POPULAR VOTE	*ELECTORAL VOTE
Abraham Lincoln	Republican	1,866,352	180
Stephen A. Douglas	Democrat (Northern)	1,375,157	12
John C. Breckinridge	Democrat (Southern)	845,763	72
John Bell	Constitutional Union	589,581	39

*ELECTORAL VOTE: the votes that determine who wins a presidential election; a candidate needs a majority of these votes, which are cast by state based on the popular vote in that state, to become president.

poor organization, Bell pulled 10 percent of the vote.

Lincoln Elected

Lincoln won the election in November. He captured only 40 percent of the popular vote—and did not receive a single vote in the ten southern states that had never even placed his name on the ballot. But he won every state in the North, giving him a huge majority in the electoral college, which decides the presidency. Abraham Lincoln would be the new president.

CHAPTER SIX

Secession

> "It is no less than
> our fixed determination to throw off a
> Government to which we have been accustomed,
> and to prove new safeguards for our future security. If any-
> thing has been decided by the elections that sent us here, it is,
> that South Carolina must dissolve her connection with the
> [Federal] Confederacy as speedily as possible."

D.F. Jamison, speaking at the South Carolina
secession convention (1860)

What Is the Union?

The question the nation faced in the winter of 1860–1861 was, what was the Union? Was it a single nation that could grow—as new territories and states joined—but not shrink? Or was a federation of separate states that ould come and go as they pleased?

This question arose because, start-ing in December 1861, the Southern states followed up years of threats and began to leave the Union. Southerners feared that Lincoln would move to end slavery—although he had never said he would do so. Many Southerners believed that they would be better off having their own country, where they could keep slavery and live in peace.

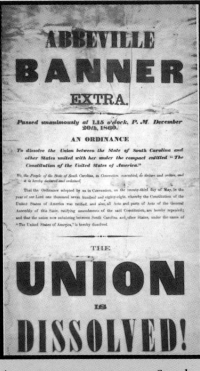

A newspaper announces South Carolina's decision to secede from the Union.

The Union Is Dissolved!

Just a few weeks after the election, a convention of South Carolina citizens met in Charleston. On December 20, 1860, the **delegates** voted 169–0 to secede. Within weeks, Mississippi, Florida, Alabama, Georgia, Louisiana, and Texas—the rest of Lower South—followed.

Eight slave states—the Upper South and the Border States—remained. Many people in these states wanted to preserve slavery, but many also hoped to preserve the Union. In votes in Virginia, North Carolina, Tennessee, and Arkansas, secession was defeated for the time being.

A New Government Forms in the South

The Southerners wanted more than simply to leave the Union. They wanted

SAM HOUSTON IN TEXAS

For many Southerners, the decision about secession was difficult and painful. Sam Houston, governor of Texas, had served as the first elected president of the Republic of Texas, after Texas won its independence from Mexico in 1836. He had always hoped that Texas would join the United States—a dream that was realized in 1845.

In 1861, though, many Texans wanted to leave the Union and join the other states of the South. Houston campaigned passionately against this idea. Then a convention of Texans voted to secede. When Houston refused to take an oath of allegiance to the new Confederate States of America, he was forced to resign.

The Secession of the South		
STATE	**REGION**	**DATE OF SECESSION**
South Carolina	Lower South	Dec. 20, 1860
Mississippi	Lower South	Jan. 9, 1861
Florida	Lower South	Jan. 10, 1861
Alabama	Lower South	Jan. 11, 1861
Georgia	Lower South	Jan. 19, 1861
Louisiana	Lower South	Jan. 26, 1861
Texas	Lower South	Feb. 1, 1861
Virginia	Upper South	Apr. 17, 1861
Arkansas	Upper South	May 6, 1861
North Carolina	Upper South	May 7, 1861
Tennessee	Upper South	May 7, 1861

EFFORTS AT COMPROMISE

Several attempts were made to resolve the secession crisis. One package of constitutional amendments offered by Senator John J. Crittenden of Kentucky reached the Senate, but Republicans defeated it because they thought it too pro-South. A peace convention met in February 1861. It revised the Crittenden amendments to make them more acceptable to the North, but even these changes were not enough. When the bills were brought to Congress, Republicans voted them down.

to create a new country of their own, separate from the North.

In February 1861, delegates from six seceded states met (Texas was not present). The delegates quickly wrote a new constitution for the Confederate States of America, which was very similar to the U.S. Constitution. One difference was that it guaranteed the protection of slavery and its extension to any new territories. It also limited the president to one term, though one of six years. Finally, the document granted that the states of the Confederacy were "sovereign and independent." This meant that each state reserved the right to leave the new nation if it wished.

The convention also chose a president—Jefferson Davis of Mississippi. Davis spoke strong words: "The South is determined to maintain her position, and make all who oppose her smell Southern powder and feel Southern steel."

The Waiting Time

Alhough he was elected in November 1860, Lincoln would not become

In his inaugural address, Jefferson Davis echoed the Declaration of Independence:

"Our present political condition has been achieved in a manner unprecedented in the history of nations. It illustrates the American idea that governments rest on the consent of the governed, and that it is the right of the people to alter or abolish them at will whenever they become destructive of the ends for which they were established."

JEFFERSON DAVIS

Born in Kentucky, Jefferson Davis grew up in Mississippi. He graduated from the U.S. Military Academy at West Point in 1828 but resigned from the army to become a planter. Though he gained great wealth, he enlisted in the army when the Mexican War broke out, and he served with distinction. In the early 1850s, he was secretary of war. Later he became a leading spokesman for the South in the Senate.

Seeing himself as a military expert, President Davis took a strong role in the Confederacy's military affairs. He tried to forge a strong central government, which angered many Southerners. He defended his actions by saying "We are fighting for independence, and that, or extermination, we will have." After the war ended, Davis spent two years in prison before being released in 1867. He died in 1889.

president until the following March. In the meantime, he directed the Republican response to the compromise ideas being debated in Congress. He also picked the men who would serve in his cabinet—including four who had fought him for the Republican nomination. People wondered what he would do about secession.

Lincoln left Illinois, for Washington, D.C., in early February. He gave many speeches along the way, but none revealed his plans.

Meanwhile, James Buchanan, who was president until March, spoke. In late December of the previous year, he had said that the southern states had no right to secede. But his message ended weakly. The national government, he said, had no power to force states to stay in the Union if they wished to leave. Buchanan also urged Northerners to reduce their criticism of slavery.

The New President Speaks

On March 4, 1861, Lincoln took the oath of office as president and finally spoke officially on the crisis facing the nation. He needed to be careful— eight slaveholding states had still not seceded. He had to make clear his belief that secession was illegal but say nothing that would lead these key states to join the Confederacy.

First, he tried to reassure the South: "I have no purpose, directly or indirectly, to interfere with the institution of slavery in the states where it exists. I believe I have no lawful right to do so, and I have no inclination to do so." But he also declared that the secession was illegal: "No state upon its own mere motion can lawfully get out of the Union . . . [and] acts of violence within any state or states against the authority of the United States are **insurrectionary**." At the same time, Lincoln promised there would be no war—"unless it be forced upon" the Union.

LINCOLN'S ARRIVAL

Lincoln's trip to Washington to be sworn in as President ended in an embarrassing way. He was warned of attempts on his life if he stopped in Baltimore, where many people favored the South. So he was taken through the city in secret, at night. The truth was soon replaced by rumors that he had skulked through the city in disguise. Soon cartoonists printed pictures making fun of him.

On March 4, 1861, Abraham Lincoln was sworn in as president of a fracturing nation. Seven states had already left the Union, and the threat remained that more would do so.

Lincoln ended his inaugural
address by trying to reconcile North and South:

"We are not enemies, but friends. We must not be enemies. Though passion may have strained, it must not break our bonds of affection. The mystic chords of memory, stretching from every battle-field, and patriot grave, to every living heart and hearthstone . . . will yet swell the chorus of the Union, when again touched, as surely they will be, by the better angels of our nature."

CHAPTER SEVEN

War!

~

The day after Union soldiers surrendered Fort Sumter, in the harbor of Charleston, South Carolina, Southerners raised their flag in the fort.

The Issue of Federal Property

In his inaugural address, Lincoln placed the ball in the Confederacy's court. While he would not accept secession, he would not start a war—Jefferson Davis would have to fire the first shot. He took this position to try to buy time, but time was running out. He had also vowed "to hold, occupy, and possess the property and places belonging to the government." That pledge cut to the heart of his first important decision.

Across the South, state governments had taken control of U.S. government buildings, such as forts and arsenals. Four southern forts remained in Union hands, though. One of them sat in the harbor of Charleston, South Carolina— Fort Sumter—a symbolic challenge that rankled Confederate leaders. They installed batteries around Charleston's harbor with cannons aimed threateningly at the fort.

Focus on Sumter

The Sumter situation was serious because the soldiers in the fort were running out of supplies. Back in January 1861, South Carolina's governor had warned that he would view attempts to send supplies to the fort as acts of war. Later that month, South Carolina fired its guns at a Union supply ship, forcing it to turn away from the fort. What would the new president do?

On March 29, 1861, Lincoln decided to resupply the fort. He sent word to South Carolina officials so they would know that a ship loaded with food for the fort's soldiers would arrive soon. The Confederates then demanded that the Union commander, Major Robert Anderson, surrender the fort. He refused. On April 12, Confederate cannons opened fire. They pounded the fort for more than thirty hours until

Though divisions would reappear later, the attack on Fort Sumter brought the North together. Lincoln's former opponent Stephen A. Douglas closed ranks with the president:

"There are only two sides to the question. Every man must be for the United States or against it. There can be no neutrals in this war, only patriots—or traitors."

Stephen A. Douglas, speech in Chicago (1861)

EDMUND RUFFIN

Edmund Ruffin was an agricultural reformer and a powerful advocate of secession. He was born into Virginia's wealthy planter class in 1794. Ruffin determined that planting the same crop every year led to poor harvests. By mixing marl with the soil and varying crops, he increased his yields. Ruffin eventually gained great influence across the South through the articles and books he wrote promoting his methods.

In the 1850s, Ruffin focused his writings on defending slavery and southern nationalism. Though in his sixties, he joined the state **militia** *that had its guns aimed at Fort Sumter. Some accounts say he fired the first shot. Four years later, after the South's defeat, he committed suicide. He left a note saying, "I cannot survive my country's liberty."*

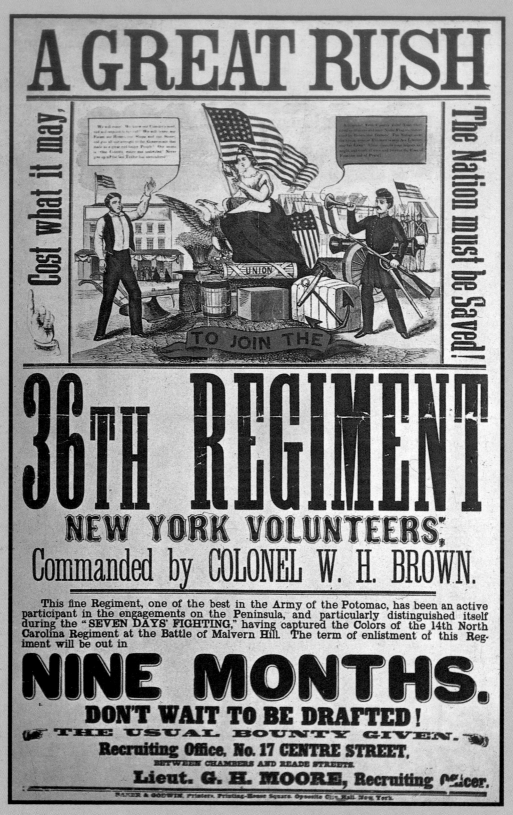

This Northern recruiting poster reveals the goal of most Northerners early in the war: "The Nation must be Saved!"

Anderson was forced to surrender. The North and South were now at war.

Lincoln Moves

Lincoln moved fast to declare that a state of rebellion existed. He asked the state governors to raise militias and send them to Washington to defend the Union. Lincoln asked for 75,000 troops. Many Northern governors promised more.

The story was different in the Upper South, however. Virginia's governor said that "the militia of Virginia will not be furnished to Washington" to fight the Southern states. The governors of North Carolina and Arkansas sent similar messages. Tennessee's governor, Isham Harris, was even more defiant: "Tennessee will not furnish a single man for purpose of coercion, but 50,000 if necessary, for the defense of our rights and those of our Southern brethren."

The Final Secession

The people of the Upper South soon showed they felt the same as their

governors. On April 17—just two days after Abraham Lincoln's call for volunteers—Virginia voted to secede. Within weeks, Arkansas, Tennessee, and North Carolina followed. The Confederacy had grown to eleven states. Soon after, the Confederates decided to move their capital from Montgomery, Alabama, to Richmond, Virginia.

Abraham Lincoln had even more worries. He knew that if the Border States left the Union, the Confederacy would grow even larger. The governor of Missouri had also refused to supply militia troops, as had the governor of Kentucky—Lincoln's birthplace. Worse, crowds of Southern sympathizers in Baltimore had harassed troops from Massachusetts who were marching through the city on their way to Washington. Lincoln had to hold onto the state of Maryland or his capital, Washington, D.C., would be surrounded by states of the Confederacy.

Mary Boykin Chesnut recorded the excitement felt in Charleston over the news of Sumter's fall:

"I did not know that one could live such days of excitement. . . Everybody tells you half of something and then rushes off to tell something else or to hear the last news. . . .In the afternoon, Mrs. Preston, Mrs. Joe Heyward, and I drove round the Battery. We were in an open carriage. What a changed scene. The very liveliest crowd I think I ever saw. Everybody talking at once."

Mary Boykin Chesnut, diary entry for April 15, 1861

CHAPTER EIGHT

Planning for War

Northern Goals and Problems

The North began the war aiming to restore the Union. To win, it would have to destroy southern armies and Southerners' desire for independence—though few Northerners realized it at the time. They believed that the war could be won quickly, simply by capturing the Confederate capital at Richmond, Virginia.

Lincoln faced several problems. He had to keep the Border States in the Union. At the same time, many of his supporters believed in abolition. If he did not end slavery, he would lose their support. But if he did free the slaves, he would lose the Border States—and perhaps the support of many northern whites as well. Another problem was that Washington, D.C., was very near the Confederacy and, thus, vulnerable to attack.

Northern Leaders

Along with a strong leader in Lincoln, the North had many talented generals. It took a long time to identify them, however, and several incompetent commanders committed costly mistakes early in the war. The interference of Congress—and sometimes of

Union generals included some who had graduated from the U.S. Military Academy at West Point and some who were prominent politicians or business leaders.

ABRAHAM LINCOLN

Tall, thin, and bony, Abraham Lincoln was often mocked for his looks and his unpol ished manner. He often suffered from depression. During the war, Lincoln agonized over the mounting casualties. He also had to endure the death of one of his children and the growing mental imbalance of his wife. Despite these difficulties, he skillfully guided the Union through the Civil War.

Born and raised in Kentucky, Lincoln was self-educated. Moving to Illinois, he worked as a store clerk and soon after won election to the state legislature. He became a lawyer and married Mary Todd, who belonged to a well-off slaveholding family from Kentucky. Originally a member of the Whig party, he opposed the Mexican War dur ing his one term in Congress.

Although he rose in society through his marriage and his political career, Lincoln remained humble and unpretentious. When elected, few Northerners realized his depth, character, or ability. Lincoln succeeded because he was a masterful politician and was completely devoted to the cause of restoring the Union. His eloquent speech es, especially his two inaugural addresses and the Gettysburg Address, remain model expresssion of the U.S. values of freedom and equality.

Lincoln—with military decisions would often plague the North.

Southern Plans and Problems

The South needed simply to convince the North to stop fighting. If the war cost the North too much in men or money, Northerners who wanted peace would gain in power and force an end to the war.

But the North had far more resources. It had twice as many people, twice the miles of railroad track, five times the number of factories, and more than one and half times more gold. To have a chance, the South needed help. A key goal, then, was to convince Britain and France to recognize its independence. With recognition could come needed supplies.

The South had two other problems. One-third of its people were slaves, who could not be counted on to fight. Finally, the South's political structure created difficulties. The weak central government could not command the resources it needed to carry out the war.

Southern Leaders

Although it lacked the material resources of the North, the South had excellent military leadership. Many of the regular U.S. Army's most able officers were from the South, and the vast

DuPont's gunpowder works, near Wilmington, Delaware, provided powder used by the North. The South had few factories to make guns and ammunition when the war began.

Thomas Crittenden, son of the senator who had tried to find a compromise to avoid war, joined the Union army. His brother George became a Confederate general.

majority resigned their commissions to join their states. Generals like Joseph E. Johnston, Stonewall Jackson, and James Longstreet would prove to be skillful fighters. Virginian Robert E. Lee was so well respected that he was offered command of the Union army. Once Virginia seceded, however, Lee turned the offer down and joined many fellow officers in resigning from the army. It would prove an important loss for the Union—as well as a major gain for the Confederacy.

BROTHER AGAINST BROTHER

The Civil War has been called a war of "brother against brother" because—despite their differences—the people of North and South shared many traits. It was even more painfully true for some families. Senator John J. Crittenden of Kentucky saw one son became a Union general and another a Confederate general. These splits even touched Lincoln's own family. Four of his wife's brothers fought for the South.

Sometimes these family conflicts took tragic turns. In the Buchanan family, a Union naval officer died when his ship was attacked by a Confederate ship commanded by his brother.

Many southern officers in the regular U.S. Army resigned their commissions to join their states. They often parted sadly from friends who remained with the Union. The commander of Fort Sumter had been the artillery instructor of the man who commanded the guns of the South. It was just the first of many examples from throughout the war in which former friends and classmates met in battle.

1787 *May–Sep.:* Constitutional Convention writes Constitution, leaves slavery legal. *July:* Northwest Ordinance bans slavery from the Old Northwest.

1820 *Mar.:* Missouri Compromise finalized.

1829 *Sep.:* Walker's *Appeal* published.

1831 *Jan.:* Garrison issues the first edition of *The Liberator.*

1832 *Nov.:* South Carolina nullifies the "Tariff of Abominations."

1833 *Feb.:* Clay engineers a compromise that solves the Nullification Crisis.

1839 *Nov.:* Abolitionists form the Liberty party to run antislavery candidates for office.

1846 *May:* Mexican War begins. *June:* United States gains Oregon Territory in treaty with Britain. *Aug.:* House approves Wilmot Proviso, banning slavery from any lands obtained in the Mexican War but the Senate does not approve it.

1848 *Mar.:* Treaty of Guadalupe Hidalgo ends Mexican War and gives United States all or part of seven states.

1849 Thousands flock to California, hoping to gain wealth in its Gold Rush.

1850 *Sep.:* Congress agrees on the Compromise of 1850. Slave catchers begin moving North to catch escaped slaves; some Northerners organize resistance.

1852 *Mar.: Uncle Tom's Cabin* published in book form.

1854 *May:* Kansas-Nebraska Act passed.

1855 Violence begins in Kansas.

1856 *May:* Brown leads antislavery forces in Pottawatomie Massacre. *May:* Brooks attacks Sumner in Senate. *Nov.:* Republicans run first candidate for president.

1857 *Mar.:* In Dred Scott decision, Supreme Court declares the Missouri Compromise unconstitutional.

1858 *Nov.:* Douglas defeats Lincoln for Illinois Senate seat.

1859 *Oct.:* Brown's raid on Harper's Ferry.

1860 *June:* Democratic party splits, with Northern and Southern candidates. *Nov.:* Lincoln wins presidential election by sweeping the North. *Dec.:* South Carolina secedes.

1861 *Jan.–Feb.:* Mississippi, Florida, Alabama, Georgia, Louisiana, Texas secede. *Feb. 18:* Jefferson Davis inaugurated as president of the Confederacy. *Mar.:* Lincoln inaugurated; decides to resupply Fort Sumter. *Apr. 12:* Fort Sumter attacked; surrenders on April 13. *Apr. 15:* Lincoln calls for volunteers. *Apr.–May:* Virginia, Arkansas, North Carolina, Tennessee secede.

Glossary

abolitionist: a person who worked to end slavery.

arsenal: a place where weapons and ammunition are stored.

autobiography: the life story of a person written by that person.

Border States: the states on the northern edge of the southern states, in which there was slavery, but it was not a very strong a part of society; including Delaware, Maryland, Kentucky, and Missouri, all of which stayed in the Union.

cash crops: farm products grown for sale rather than for the farm family to eat; important cash crops in the North and West were wheat and corn; cash crops in the South included hemp, rice, tobacco, and cotton.

delegate: a person who represents a group at a meeting.

Far West: the regions west of the Mississippi River that were still sparsely settled by whites in 1860, including the present-day states of North and South Dakota, Nebraska, Kansas, Oklahoma, New Mexico, Colorado, Wyoming, Montana, Idaho, Utah, Arizona, California, Nevada, Oregon, and Washington.

immigrant: a person who comes to a new country to live permanently.

insurrectionary: revolting against an authority or government.

manifest destiny: the belief that the United States would expand across the continent to the Pacific Ocean.

militia: A military unit containing citizens who volunteer for duty on a temporary basis.

North: the free states north of Maryland and the Ohio River, including New England (Maine, New Hampshire, Vermont, Massachusetts, Rhode Island, and Connecticut); New York; New Jersey; Pennsylvania; the Old Northwest (Ohio, Michigan, Indiana, Illinois, Wisconsin, and Minnesota); and Iowa.

Old Northwest: the states that emerged from the Northwest Territories that were formed in the 1780s, including Ohio, Indiana, Illinois, Michigan, Wisconsin, and Minnesota.

plantation: at the time of the Civil War, large farm owned by Southern whites where enslaved African Americans worked to grow cotton or other crops for export.

sabotage: to damage property or materials deliberately.

secede: to formally withdraw from an organization.

sectional: regional or local.

South: the slaveholding states, including the Border States (Delaware, Maryland, Kentucky, and Missouri); the Upper South (Virginia, North Carolina, Tennessee, and Arkansas); and the Lower South (South Carolina, Georgia, Florida, Alabama, Mississippi, Louisiana, and Texas).

tariff: sum added to the cost of goods imported from another country.

Further Resources

These books and web sites cover the events leading up to the Civil War and the people who shaped those events:

WEB SITES

www.civilwarhome.com/ Civilwar.com web site.

www.pbs.org/wgbh/amex/lincolns/ The Time of the Lincolns web site.

lcweb2.loc.gov/ammem/aaohtml/ exhibit/aointro.html African American Odyssey web site.

members.aol.com/jfepperson/causes.html Causes of the Civil War web site.

BOOKS

Bolotin, Norman. *The Civil War A to Z : A Young Reader's Guide to over 100 People, Places, and Points of Importance.* New York: Dutton, 2002.

Clinton, Catherine. *Scholastic Encyclopedia of the Civil War.* New York: Scholastic Books, 1999.

Editors of Time-Life. *The Time-Life History of the Civil War.* New York: Barnes and Noble Books, 1995.

Erickson, Paul. *Daily Life on a Southern Plantation.* New York: Puffin Books, 2000.

Herda, D.J. *The Dred Scott Case: Slavery and Citizenship.* Hillside, J.D.: Enslow, 1994.

Katz, William Loren. *Breaking the Chains: African-American Slave Resistance.* New York: Aladdin Paperbacks, 1998.

Lutz, Norma Jean. *The History of the Republican Party.* Philadelphia: Chelsea House, 2000.

Smith, Carter, ed. *Prelude to War: A Sourcebook on the Civil War.* Brookfield, Conn: Millbrook Press, 1993.

Yancey, Diane. *Leaders of the North and South.* San Diego: Lucent Books, 2000.

Zdrok-Ptaszek, ed. *The Antislavery Movement.* San Diego: Greenhaven Press, 2002.

Index

Page numbers in *italics* indicate maps and diagrams.